Ten
abo

C000299634

ex libris

Candlestick Press

Published by:
Candlestick Press,
Diversity House, 72 Nottingham Road, Arnold, Nottingham UK NG5 6LF
www.candlestickpress.co.uk

Design and typesetting by Diversity Creative Marketing Solutions Ltd.,
www.diversity.agency

Printed by Ratcliff & Roper Print Group, Nottinghamshire, UK

Selection and Introduction © Ian Duhig, 2018

Cover illustration © Ian Phillips, 2018 www.reliefprint.co.uk

Candlestick Press monogram © Barbara Shaw, 2008

© Candlestick Press, 2018

ISBN 978 1 907598 63 0

Acknowledgements:

The poems in this pamphlet are reprinted from the following books, all by
permission of the publishers listed unless stated otherwise. Every effort has
been made to trace the copyright holders of the poems published in this book.
The editor and publisher apologise if any material has been included without
permission or without the appropriate acknowledgement, and would be glad to be
told of anyone who has not been consulted. Thanks are due to all the copyright
holders cited below for their kind permission:

Eavan Boland, *New Selected Poems* (Carcanet; W. W. Norton, 2014)

Kayo Chingonyi, *Kumukanda* (Chatto & Windus, 2017)

Ian Duhig, poem first published in this anthology

Philip Gross, *The Water Table* (Bloodaxe Books, 2007)
www.bloodaxebooks.com

Kathleen Jamie, *The Overhaul* (Picador, 2012) by kind permission of the author

Zaffar Kunial, poem first published in this anthology, by kind permission of the
author

Beth McDonough, *A Bee's Breakfast* (Beautiful Dragons Collaborations, 2017)

Eiléan Ní Chuilleanáin, *The Girl who Married the Reindeer* (The Gallery Press,
2001) by kind permission of the author and The Gallery Press, Loughcrew,
Oldcastle, County Meath, Ireland

Pascale Petit, *Mama Amazonica* (Bloodaxe Books, 2017)
www.bloodaxebooks.com

Julian Turner, *Planet Struck* (Anvil, 2011) by kind permission of Carcanet Press

All permissions cleared courtesy of Swift Permissions
(swiftpermissions@gmail.com)

Where poets are no longer living, their dates are given.

Contents

Introduction

"The river is everywhere" wrote Hermann Hesse in 'Siddartha' so this anthology celebrates what is in many ways a universal metaphor. There are wonderful traditions of river poetry all over the world – rivers inevitably symbolise communication, as in our own cliché of 'babbling' brooks. They are also beautiful, of course, which is also why they continue to enjoy the notice of poets.

Rivers sculpted Yorkshire's karst landscape which in Julian Turner's stunning 'Appletreewick' threatens a return to the waters from which all land first rose. Beth McDonough's 'Tribute' is a joyous song invoking the word 'tributary' with which the Tay is so richly fed, again now by her fresh words. If Kathleen Jamie's 'Springs' strikes a note of despair at our abuse of rivers, it is a call to action as well as wonderful writing.

Rivers can also be seen as the bloodstreams of countries and some of the poems explore their ecological, social and political significance. Zaffar Kunial's poem '*from* Empty Words' tenderly negotiates its course through a complex heritage of language and love, via particular rivers. My own poem 'An Aroko for David Oluwale' evokes a darker legacy, exploring the river as an instrument of murder.

In the course of the selection we also encounter iconic rivers including the Amazon, the Liffey (whose name in Irish means *Life*) and the Loire. Finally we arrive at the Severn which carries us all the way to the sea of humanity and language.

Rivers are givers of life, endlessly changing and recycling. We hope that you will find plenty to relish in this intriguing selection and that your own life will be enriched by spending time in the invigorating company of water on the move.

Ian Duhig

Appletreewick

Everywhere the water's height
surprises, a great smooth swelling
over weirs, a sheer glass welling
above the banks as skeins of light
wind around themselves in mauves
and greys, the bearded islets broken
from the shores by the red churn
chafed with the white of rock-cleaved waves,
as if it had transformed the soft
rise of the ground to liquid, the scuff
of pasture rippling on the bones
of rock like shot silk, while the rafts
of farms, roped to their mooring stones
by walls, ride on a tide of turf.

Julian Turner

Tribute
To Keir and the Tay

Fresh, smiling; you are miles upstream.
Helmeted, jacketed, roped
against the force full Lochay
or Dochart, soon to tumble, cascade
join Loch Tay, then stream out
swallow that naughty Braan. Perhaps
you'll paddle in some other pooling,
ready to push Glen Ogle past
ghost trains, still in peatbrown
Loch Earn. Now leave Saint Fillan's
chuckle through birks, under rodden, then
spill... flood all the fields
by Auchterarder, meet the long tide
at Newburgh's ebb.
Here, low in the waiting
calm of the black-walled Ferry harbour
I float, blink in salt.

Beth McDonough

from Empty Words

Full-rhyme with Jhelum
the river nearest his home –
my father's 'realm'.

*

Near one grandfather –
Stan, no stone above his head –
Warwickshire's Anker.

*

Herefordshire's Lugg –
stone's throw from Mum – 'bright' like lux
and distant luck.

*

– then melts forever
Burns's snow glows bright longer
here, on the Calder.

*

a momentary stay
I played near the Cole, no glints
from the Calder, here.

*

Stratford-on-Avon
Mum and Dad's first date. Never
found out where they went.

Zaffar Kunial

Springs

Full March moon and gale-force easters, the pair of them
sucking and shoving the river
back into its closet in the hills, or trying to. Naturally

the dykes failed, the town's last fishing boat
raved at the pier-head, then went down; diesel-
corrupted water cascaded into front-yards, coal-holes, garages,

and *there's naethin ye can dae,*
said the old boys, the sages, which may be true; but river –
what have you left us? Evidence of an inner life, secrets
of your estuarine soul hawked halfway

up Shore Street, up East and Mid Shore, and arrayed
in swags all through the swing-park: plastic trash and broken reeds,
driftwood, bust TVs . . .
              and a salmon,
dead, flung beneath the see-saw, the crows are onto at once.

Kathleen Jamie

An Aroko for David Oluwale

Oluwale is Yoruba for *'God Has Come Home'*
but he came to find Hell in God's Own Country,
no home but cold Leeds streets or police cells,
in his asylum only electro-convulsive therapy.

Now by the Aire, where David drowned fleeing
policemen's boots, his feet light from hunger,
my small nomadic cowrie garden grows for one
who'd grown to be a shell of himself in this city.

An empty cowrie is full as an egg with meanings:
Gods' eyes, they make *arokos*, magic messages.
Because *efa*, Yoruba for six, has the same letters
as the word to draw, my six cowries set down here

draw David's Christian ghost into Oshun's arms,
water Goddess with a name of water, that he too
might step into the true meaning of his own name
borne back to Africa where the river of us all rose.

This alchemy of cold fire on the Aire's earth makes
nothing happen, like poetry, yet makes something
from nothing for a man treated like he was nothing,
making room to reflect on river water running softly.

Ian Duhig

The Scar

Dawn on the river.
Dublin rises out of what reflects it:

Anna Liffey
looks to the east, to the sea,
her profile carved out by the light
on the old Carlisle bridge.

I was five
when a piece of glass
cut my head and left a scar.
Afterwards my skin felt different.

And still does on these autumn days when
the mist hides the city
from the Liffey.

The Liffey hides
the long ships, the muskets and the burning domes.

Everything but this momentary place.
And those versions of the Irish rain
which change the features
of a granite face.

If colony is a wound what will heal it?
After such injuries
what difference do we feel?

No answer in the air,
on the water, in the distance.
And yet

Emblem of this old,
torn and traded city,
altered by its river, its weather,
I turn to you as if there were –

one flawed head towards another.

Eavan Boland

The Jaguar

Como un río de tigres enterrados
– Pablo Neruda, 'Alturas de Macchu Picchu'

He lay on driftwood, the river below him
as if he had cast it off –

the apricot river rosetted
with the pads of waterlilies,
its nap lifted by a dawn breeze.

His whiskers were old as horsetails,
his lashes ferns bordering
the swamps of his eyes.

I crouched in my boat –
no one had been here before,
I would not come again.

The forest swayed with tattoos
of dark and light, no and yes.

And everywhere there were eyes,
rainclouds of eyes, terror-struck,

as if the first human opened hers
and saw mist rising
from her mother's flanks.

My baby self saw the archangel-beast,
the one who arrived to help
with my birth,

> whose irises are hoar forests,
> whose teeth are the pain-price,
> whose roar is the earth
> > opening its gates,

the boat of my skin rocking
its hallelujahs,
as it navigated the passage
through and away from Mama.

Like a river of buried jaguars,
the day said,
> *a river you have to dive into*
> *and swim the length of,*
> *squeezing between the corpses.*

Pascale Petit

Crossing the Loire

I saluted the famous river as I do every year
Turning south as if the plough steered,
Kicking, at the start of a new furrow, my back
To the shady purple gardens with benches under plum trees
By the river that hunts between piers and sandbanks –

I began threading the long bridge, I bowed my head
And lifted my hands from the wheel for an instant of trust,
I faced the long rows of vines curving up the hillside
Lightly like feathers, and longer than the swallow's flight,
My road already traced before me in a dance

Of three nights and three days,
Of sidestepping hills and crescent lights blinding me
(If there was just a bar counter and ice and a glass, and a room upstairs:
But it rushed past me and how many early starts before
The morning when the looped passes descend to the ruined arch?)

She came rising up out of the water, her eyes were like sandbanks
The wrinkles in her forehead were like the flaws in the mist
(Maybe a long narrow boat with a man lying down
And a rod and line like a frond of hair dipping in the stream)
She was humming the song about the estuary, and the delights
Of the salt ocean, the lighthouse like a summons; and she told me:

The land will not go to that measure, it lasts, you'll see
How the earth widens and mountains are empty, only
With tracks that search and dip, from here to the city of Rome
Where the road gallops up to the dome as big as the sun.

You will see your sister going ahead of you
And she will not need to rest, but you must lie
In the dry air of your hotel where the traffic grinds before dawn,
The cello changing gear at the foot of the long hill,

And think of the story of the suitors on horseback
Getting ready to trample up the mountain of glass.

Eiléan Ní Chuilleanáin

Baltic Mill

Though you maintain the elements
have conspired against us we still
inch the cobbled street past Castle
Keep down to the Quayside's rain-
slick paving slabs all for the thrill
of standing across from Baltic Mill
in a turbid mist lifted from the Tyne.

We planned to catch a talk at the Laing
or the Biscuit but, pushed for time,
plumped for a backstreet pizzeria, throw-
back to another world, a haberdasher's
maybe or greasy spoon for blackface
minstrels from Gateshead mines and
iron works. The North Sea wind-chill

bids us leave behind this city of faces
cast in stories passed down, vestige
of years when hundreds of miles stood
between us. The exact course that brought
us here is unimportant. It is that we met
like this river, drawn from two sources,
offered up our flaws, our sedimental selves.

Kayo Chingonyi

Severn Song
(for John Karl Gross)

The Severn was brown and the Severn was blue –
not this-then-that, not either-or,
no mixture. Two things can be true.
The hills were clouds and the mist was a shore.

The Severn was water, the water was mud
whose eddies stood and did not fill,
the kind of water that's thicker than blood.
The river was flowing, the flowing was still,

the tide-rip the sound of dry fluttering wings
with waves that did not break or fall.
We were two of the world's small particular things.
We were old, we were young, we were no age at all,

for a moment not doing, nor coming undone –
words gained, words lost, till who's to say
which was the father, which was the son,
a week, or fifty years, away.

But the water said *earth* and the water said *sky*.
We were everyone we'd ever been or would be,
every angle of light that says *You*, that says *I*,
and the sea was the river, the river the sea.

Philip Gross